INDIAN SINGING
IN 20TH
CENTURY AMERICA

The publication of this book was supported with grants from the National Endowment for the Arts, the Oregon Arts Commission, and the Oregon Institute of Literary Arts.

Cover art *Transforming Star*
Mixed media fiber sculpture by Gail Tremblay.
Cover design and book design by Debbie Berrow.

Calyx Books are distributed to the trade by The Talman Company Inc., 150 Fifth Ave., NY, NY 10011, 212-620-3182. Calyx Books are also available through major library distributors and jobbers and most small press distributors including: Airlift, Bookpeople, Bookslinger, Inland Book Co., Pacific Pipeline, and Small Press Distribution. For personal orders or other information write: Calyx Books, PO Box B, Corvallis, OR 97339, 503-753-9384.

Library of Congress Cataloging-in-Publication Data
Tremblay, Gail.
    Indian singing in 20th century America: poetry / by Gail Tremblay.
        p.   cm.
    ISBN 0-934971-14-5 :(alk.paper) $16.95.—ISBN 0-934971-13-7
(pbk.) :(alk.paper) $8.95
    1. Indians of North America—Poetry. I. Title. II. Title:
Indian singing in twentieth century America.
PS3570.R38515   1989
811'.54—dc20   89-22374
                                                                                       CIP

Printed in the U.S.A.

INDIAN SINGING IN 20ᵀᴴ CENTURY AMERICA

GAIL TREMBLAY

CALYX BOOKS
Corvallis, Oregon

The author wishes to thank the following publications in which these poems were previously published:

"After the Invasion," "Drum," "Gathering Basket Grass," "'Ohgi' we," and "Sehià:rak" were published in *New Voices from the Longhouse* (Greenfield Review Press, 1989). "American Abroad," "Crow Voices," and "Night Gives Old Woman the Word" were published in *Night Gives Woman the Word* (F limited Gallery, 1979). "American Abroad," "Bus Ride, Omaha, 1977," "Crow Voices," "Gathering Basket Grass," "Grandfather Dancing," "Huckleberry Feast, Warm Springs Nation, 1979," "Night Gives Old Woman the Word," and "Relocation" were published in *Talking to the Grandfathers* (Annex 21 #3, University of Nebraska, Omaha, 1981). "Bus Ride, Omaha, 1977" and "Relocation" were published in *Sandhills and Other Geographies* (Sandhills Press, 1980). "Coyote, Hanging in a Museum, Comes off the Wall," "It is important.," "Light Shakes," and "The Returning" were published in *Dancing on the Rim of the World: An Anthology of Contemporary Northwest Native American Writing* (Sun Tracks Press, forthcoming). "Crow Voices," "Gathering Basket Grass," and "Night Gives Old Woman the Word" were published in *The Denver Quarterly* (University of Denver Press, 1980). "Crow Voices" was also published in *The 1981 Anthology of Magazine Verse and Yearbook of American Poetry* (Monitor Book Company, Inc., 1981). "Fall," "To Joseph, who is never gone:," "Laughter Breaks," "Wake," and "The Women Faculty and Staff Ride Home from British Columbia" were published in *The Wooster Review* (Wooster College, 1979). "Falling, Gloria Looks Up" was published in *Women and Aging, An Anthology by Women* (Calyx Books, 1986). "Indian Singing in 20th Century America," "Singing Out the Ghosts," and "Tsooyes Beach, Makah Nation, 1981" were published in *A Nation Within* (Outrigger Press, 1983). "Indian Singing in 20th Century America," "Medicine Bearer," "Night Gives Old Woman the Word," and "Reflections on a Visit to the Burke Museum, University of Washington, Seattle" were published in *Harper's Anthology of 20th Century Native American Poetry* (Harper & Row, 1987). "Night Gives Old Woman the Word" was published in *Maize (Centro Cultural de la Raza*, 1979). "To Joseph, who is never gone:" was published in *The Wooster Review* (Wooster College, 1988). "Urban Indians: Pioneer Square, Seattle" was published in *Bearing Witness/Sobreviviendo, Calyx, A Journal of Art and Literature by Women*, Volume 8, no.2, 1984 and *Florilegia* (Calyx Books, 1987).

This book is dedicated to my good friends whose love sustains me, and especially to Lillian Pitt, Joe Feddersen, Liz Woody, William F. Blauvelt, Hisami Yoshida, Laurette Chasé, Dean Hayasaka, Hulleah Tsinhnahjinnie, Teresa Harlan, Michio Teshima, Stan Shikuma, Tracy Lai, Barbara Thomas, Patricia Trudell-Gordon, and all the Indian Youth of America staff and campers with whom I ever worked. The rest of you know who you are, and it is your love, each and all of you, that makes life a rich experience worth writing one's way through.

I want to thank Melanie Bartmess and Jan Stentz for their help typing this manuscript and all the staff at *Calyx* for their careful proofing, editing, and work on design. I especially want to thank Margarita Donnelly, Managing Editor, for her support and interest in my book from the day I handed it over to her outside the Book Room at Bumbershoot through the long process of acceptance and publication. And to friends who commented on the work while I was writing, and people who responded at readings, and editors of periodicals and anthologies who have requested and published my work and kept me writing, thanks a lot. All of you made this book possible.

Table of Contents

Poetry

Art

FOREWORD

Gail Tremblay's work sings with the bone-chilling beauty of a siren's song. Like that song, these poems pull on ancient chants as surely as the sea might pull us back to our watery beginnings. The collection opens to a sort of beauteous mystery of a larger world, its natural order detailed with a storyteller's finesse. In the second half of the manuscript, language and imagery are more intimate, delicate as the *murmurs / that inhabit me until I learn it's sound not sense / that fills the world.* Throughout the manuscript, there is an ease of tone that allows the reader to move from laughter and joy to sorrow. And when the images evoke tears, they come with a sudden and surprising familiarity that takes the reader's breath as surely as laughter. In these poems, Tremblay draws on a world that lives, dies, lives again in a cycle where *the planet turns / the universe continues to expand.* Repeatedly, there is a timelessness about work, the use of images that are both ancient and new. These poems contain a fine music that *feeds the muscle of the heart and makes love possible.*

COLLEEN J. McELROY

PREFACE

Indian Singing in 20th Century America is a book of poems about finding ways to endure in a confused world. It celebrates cultures that understand the need for ceremony and that respect the Earth as the supporter of life. These poems are based in old traditions rooted in the American continent and even when they talk of personal matters are informed by the experience of indigenous ways of seeing. They are, however, clearly planted in contemporary American experience and record the survival of a people who continue to show strength even though they often face great loss and adversity. The book celebrates the natural world because it is that great circle of things that makes life possible. It talks of the need to stop trying to explain and excuse greed, exploitation, and murder as part of a natural order rather than an imbalance of it. In these poems, I am trying to speak of maintaining a conscious way of living on the Earth—a way that will not work toward creating the end of the world, but that talks of human beings adjusting to the constant change in the universe by finding ways to be in harmony with that change. These are also the poems of a personal experience, of conversations had and overheard which reveal how humans cope or find it hard to cope with the things that happen in their lives. In this book people experience loss of love, illness, and death and find ways to survive, to maintain their humanity, their ability to love. Perhaps because so many corn-planting, indigenous peoples know one can create a better world if communities of people are brave enough to be vulnerable, to love and give, even in this hard world where one will definitely experience loss, they have developed cultures that have informed us that a generous, caring world is possible. It is those cultures that these ancestors, thinking of the welfare of people seven generations in the future, have passed down, those cultures and that vision which I long for and struggle for and attempt to honor in this book.

GAIL TREMBLAY
August 6, 1989

INDIAN SINGING IN 20th CENTURY AMERICA

We wake; we wake the day,
the light rising in us like sun—
our breath a prayer brushing
against the feathers in our hands.
We stumble out into streets;
patterns of wires invented by strangers
are strung between eye and sky,
and we dance in two worlds,
inevitable as seasons in one,
exotic curiosities in the other
which rushes headlong down highways,
watches us from car windows, explains
us to its children in words
that no one could ever make
sense of. The image obscures
the vision, and we wonder
whether anyone will ever hear
our own names for the things
we do. Light dances in the body,
surrounds all living things—
even the stones sing
although their songs are infinitely
slower than the ones we learn
from trees. No human voice lasts

long enough to make such music sound.
Earth breath eddies between factories
and office buildings, caresses the surface
of our skin; we go to jobs, the boss
always watching the clock to see
that we're on time. He tries to shut
out magic and hopes we'll make
mistakes or disappear. We work
fast and steady and remember
each breath alters the composition
of the air. Change moves relentless,
the pattern unfolding despite their planning—
we're always there—singing round dance
songs, remembering what supports
our life—impossible to ignore.

RELOCATION

Need made the move inevitable.
The careful plans, the accidents of choice
made by strangers made it certain
that there would not be food
to share with all the neighbors who were
hungry and still be food to keep
the family alive. Packing the belongings
was difficult; none of us desired to leave
this ground made of our mothers' flesh
and bones, to go live among strangers
who buried dirt under concrete and macadam—
who, without consideration, ripped the soil
from the surface of the planet and rearranged
the elements to make toys that would be
useless in a year. Friends told us they would
visit, and we felt the sorrow of knowing
how difficult, how unlikely a journey
that would be. Loneliness welled up in us;
we felt like the gander after its mate
has been shot, our minds circling the place
where for generations we have guarded our dead
and sang the mourning songs that echo what
we've lost. We moved away, went to a city
in the center of the continent and found
no work that could delight our hands
or stimulate our minds. We struggled
to see the magic in the land—to find
the plants that healed. The neon lights
of bar signs made it difficult to see
the stars, to know the seasons
when the ceremonies must be held.
And then, by luck an old friend
from back home who had been visiting
relatives in the North, stopped—gave
gifts: feathers and a dismembered claw

taken from the corpse of a hawk—
talons sharp and digits too reminiscent
of finger bones for anyone to ever
completely relax in their presence.
Even the inanimate remains spoke
of the magic that makes objects fit
for use in ritual. We heard
the power song echo at the raw
edges of the severed skin, scaly
narrow covering that attracted light,
exploded in vision—traced
in electric lines the body of a bird.
We moved in the spirit realm that keeps
our people whole. We sat celebrating
the permanence of our connection
that shimmered at the edge
of every object in the entire
        Breathing World.

TO GROW SANE

Pain rises like a wave from an ocean
that spreads further than eye can see—
it is impossible to avoid being swallowed
by sorrow, impossible to ignore the salt
stinging even in the oldest wounds. Memory
drags the beloved dead that nothing would save
from burial grounds, from common graves,
from jars and glass cases where students
who dissected them pickled or displayed
the remains. We examine lost loves
and remember so many tender moments
locked in time—our hearts should beat
wildly then rock shut, but still we breathe
and pulse feeds the wailing brain—witness
to the violence that haunts us 'til death
seems sweeter than the madness in our world.

So often it seems unfair that we can give
everything we have and never fill the bellies
of the starving, never heal the bodies burned
and broken by bombs. The Earth's sweet fruit,
the tender shoots of plants grow while we love
and love and wake the magic that lives
in the first simple light which fills so many
birds with song. How can it be that torture,
murder, the building of instruments for death
goes on and on and on. Millions starve
while a few hoard wheat and rice and corn.
It is hard to imagine how such madness
ever began. The hunger for kindness becomes
insatiable; we no longer understand why needless
violence is defined as part of human nature.

We pray old lies will die; that visions
will dance on the land, that we will
learn a song to heal the Earth and bless
the four directions, the five colors
of people and of corn. That everyone,
black, white, yellow, red, and mixed
will see the sacred light that weaves
creation into a dazzling pattern
where life is supported by the interaction
of every creature the force that created
thinks of. We stand on the beach
by the edge of the water and weep,
let grief wash the madness away
until we see the beauty in the sun.
Light wakes us from life's nightmare, and we sing.

AMERICAN ABROAD

Only after long journeys to too many places
In too few days, through too many time zones,
Do I come to this buzzing exhaustion, weeping
In my beer in Southampton or tea in Cherbourg
At the Café Theâtre on the square.
Then for a moment I stop the world and hold time
Shut in my mind, hawks circling Buckhorn Mountain,
Grandfather praying, an eagle feather in his hand.

Tomorrow, perhaps, I will leave my job, my camera,
In one of these foreign places—
Travel inland over America, breakfast at the bus stop
In Vernal, Utah; walk across the dry land
To the center of the reservation, strip, paint
My body for prayer
And wait for the world to shift on its axis.

CROW VOICES

On the Plains, crows speak in raucous caws,
circling cornfields waiting for the weeding
woman to turn her back. In those open
spaces, their voices seem brazen
as they fly along highways looking
for the dead to pick clean to the bone—
devouring the remains, maggots and all.
Fat on road meat and grain, crows seem
always ready to play tricks, to outwit
themselves quicker than Coyote,
to gossip with Magpie, to gather light
and shine black against the sky.

In western Washington, crows speak
in steady, conversational tones, voices
muted as they convene meetings
among cedars. Speaking of spells,
they fly through mist—dark shadows
drawing dark to themselves like shamans
preparing some incredible magic
to frighten evil. Inside the rain forest,
crows act serious, whispering about enemies,
about food supplies, about how Raven
stole their wit when he proved
he was so clever he could take the sun.

COYOTE, HANGING IN A MUSEUM, COMES OFF THE WALL

for Harry Fonseca

After days of blue-haired ladies commenting
on the odd slant of your eyes, asking
if real men wear earrings, or, "darling,
perhaps he's supposed to be a pirate";
after hearing, "my, what big teeth
you have," as if all people's stories
are the same, Coyote gets lonely
for brown women whose grandfathers
told them tales, whose memories
collect adventures that run deep in time
when everything was changeable.
Coyote waits 'til no one is looking,
comes off the wall to check out other
rooms. Hoping he's found the girl
of his dreams, ripe and ready,
he laps the ass of a Maillol bronze
and sniffs the air. The hard, cold surface
caresses no one's tongue, makes him
wish for desert girls who sing
while they grind corn, who know they own
the world and shyly catch the image
of a stare in the corners of their eyes.
How was it that he ever let that bright-eyed,
brown man with the wild hair talk him
into posing, tell him fame would make them
both rich; one has to laugh, mangy gambler;
one has to laugh at where vanity and wealth
will take one. An Indian understands
you're just a horny devil playing tricks
on yourself and making the whole world
rich with ironies while people try to figure
out what the image you're creating means.

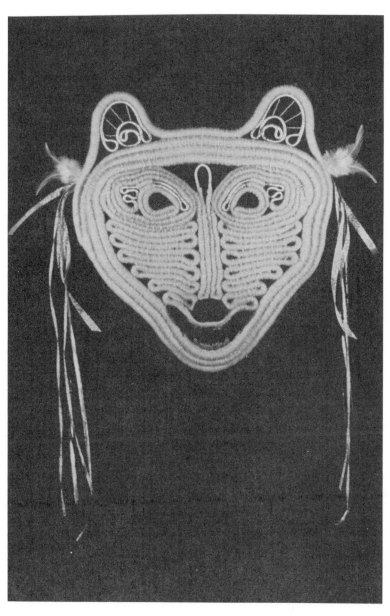

Coyote Brushes His Teeth and Goes Courting

LAUGHTER BREAKS

Laughter breaks like sun rising;
the whole world shimmers and light
shakes as though the belly of Earth
moves with the mirth in one's own gut.
The power to celebrate excess wakes in us;
we know enough to joke around, to survive
the agonies of feeling irreversible pain
explode upon the day. We sing of folly
that shapes experience, remember
to act indelicate and play. Coyote,
mangy as ever, grins and whispers
our sisters' names; he plots to climb
into the sky and dance with stars
down some eternal day. We giggle
like children, grateful that fool
never did learn to behave. Life
carries us down a stream that gurgles
between rocks and sings improbable
songs. Who cares we'll have to paddle
like hell and know panic before we get home.
That's how all the good stories were born.

DRUM

for Bill Blauvelt

Its ancient rhythms call us to our feet
and bid us move in circles on the Earth
which, turning, circles round the sun
as surely as we move around the drum.
Drum, sacred circle, gift given by a tree
carved by human hands to make the hollow
form that resonates, fills space with steady
sounds of sticks pounded against skin,
gift of horned ones who chose to let the hunter
sacrifice their flesh. Two beings who lived
and grew embraced their death so music
could be born; their spirits feed the magic
caught in song. Transformation wakes us;
we know the voice that measures out the time
so we can dance. Patterns grow until they shape
the air, alter pulse and feed the breathing
brain. Drumbeat rattles bones inside the ear.
Vibration shakes the light; creation hears.

GRANDFATHER DANCING

for Peter Ernest

The cry intrudes on dreams—
a band of false-face dancers hobbles in.
The man who keeps them, calls them,
leads them to a stove that heats a house.
Beings with twisted, wooden faces
stare, eyepieces shiny as dimes
gleaming in the light. The child
I was stares back, watching
the humpbacked ones stumble,
fall, crawl on all fours,
ragged, clothing polishing the floors.

I listen, a man says words;
tobacco, offered in the fire, burns.
Turtle rattles are struck—a sudden sound
that echoes in the hollows of their shells.
The air, already magic, feeds the lungs.
Expectation dances out of joint;
anything can happen in this room—
miracles are waiting to be born.

False-face men stand, reach
into the stove. Fire touches flesh—
nobody burns. False-face men grasp
the glowing coals, blow hot ash—
breath creating wind. People flecked
with soot give up their pain;
synapses snap, the living nerve awakes.
The band begins to dance around
the room. People join
and, with the dancers, turn—
a motion, potent, like fire in the sun.

Grandfather, you carved these beings'
faces from the trees. You wore a mask
to dance away disease. You held
the coals, blew ash on people's heads.
You gave your body to beings, and they lived.
Often, I wondered where you went when the dancers came,
and while you danced, what creature bore your name.

'OHGI' WE

Gifts of cloth and food are gathered; women meet
and name the night for feasting with the ancients
who've come before and by their loving handed
down the ways that make the nation constant
as the seasons of the year. The women send the men
to call the people in; the graveyard is restored,
the longhouse prepared to welcome the dead
who join relations to hear the words that come
before and remind us to be grateful for the patterns
of creation that make the circle whole. Tobacco
offered in the fire makes ancestors glad; smoke
rises, is accepted by the spirits in the air. The dead
join with the living to dance around the drum
that sings when beaten as surely as the people
whose voices know the rhythm that makes motion
celebration shared by generations stretching back
beyond the memory of the ones who shape the sound;
men carry out the kettle while the people spiral
round. Outside, darkness hovers; moon journeys
across sky cold with winter coming; frost fills
the empty fields. Inside, the fires burn and warm
the spirits of old ones whose bones lay
like buried treasures in the earth rooting humans
to the dirt that supports their lives. Women call
their brothers to help hand out the food. The dead
feast with descendants who share the gifts
of gardens whose plants keep them alive. People
eat with ones so old no one remembers names
and with those whose loved ones mourn; the link
travelling in the blood of those just born
that binds them to lovers having children
before the great law came to Earth and filled
the mind with peace. When the dead are full,
the dance resumes. The drummer plays the ancient
songs; ancestors remembering are glad some things

never change and whirl in stately steps timed
to the beat that vibrates to the corners of the room.
Before the first light, the women give bundles
of cloth, handing out gifts in memory of the ancients
who will go about well dressed; the dancers,
singers, cooks will make new shirts; the drum
receives a handkerchief; the drummer plays half the songs
again to make dance possible. The dead dance
and await the dawn. When first light comes,
the people prepare to raise up their arms,
and in procession, they follow the drum
outdoors where the dead can snatch scorched
cakes out of their hands seen by the rising sun,
a gift to keep ancestors fed for half the year. The living,
careful not to fall so no one dies too soon, help
the dead to bear the cakes away; reverence
and love outlive the grave; these gifts care
for ghosts who, in their day, thought seven
generations that will come must feel the good
effects of what they did. The final song is sung;
the drum grows silent, gives up its skin;
the drumstick finds the fire, dissolves to ash.
The final words are spoken inside the room;
the dead are grateful; the living return home.

¹*Ohgi´we:* Iriquois ceremony for the dead.

SEHIÀ:RAK

Always the memories come rising like smoke
from burning fields, from smoldering towns—
the soldiers whose grandfathers came from Europe
destroying hundred weights of corn, torching
storehouses of dry beans, orchards of nut trees,
fruit trees, and every longhouse they could find.
The sacred objects and household tools turn
to ash as the newcomers try to obliterate our words,
to write the history of a continent where no one
lived, a place they claim—they wish
even our ancestors' bones that make this ground
to become their heritage. They create myths
in which we disappear and make us study them
in school. Their teachers tell our children to be ashamed
of our old ones, our old ones who say:
"Thó nonkwá ionsasewe' tsi nisewaweiennó:ten."
"Sehià:rak nitesewehtahkwen."
They say our words sound funny, ridicule us
for thinking in ways they cannot understand.
They report we are too much like our savage parents.
In boarding schools, they tell us, "Don't let
your people hold you back." And, "Earth
is no one's mother; we have dominion over it."
They tear and dig and destroy, build bigger
and more awesome instruments with which to kill.
Always the memories come rising like smoke
from death camps and bombed cities; it no longer
surprises us the world is mad; images
tear up the pages and speech grows raw.
The grief wells up in us and overwhelms
our tears. To forget is to become part of a lie;
to forget is impossible. Even the maggots
are part of the sacred circle, devouring the rot,

cleaning the earth; even the maggots can
teach us to survive. We struggle to grow,
to grow corn, to feed the people,
to keep the dream of peace alive.

Sehià:rak: Remember it.
Thó nonkwá ionsasewe' tsi nisewaweiennó:ten: That way go back there to
your culture.
Sehià:rak nitesewehtahkwen: Remember it your belief.

URBAN INDIANS, PIONEER SQUARE, SEATTLE

Walking the streets, we watch the people stare,
then quickly look away when they see us notice
them. It is not always easy being watched.
At times, we hunger to be invisible, to disappear
into the crowd the way a deer can disappear
in the brush and rest for half a day. We sit
on park benches and stay still as owls hiding
in barn rafters; once in a while we blink,
but one can barely see us breathe. We know
the tourists think we're drunks—we've been out
of work so long, eating in soup kitchens, sleeping
in missions—our clothes are ragged; our shoes
are worn. Sometimes, we do find money
and drink, pretend to be happy—on good days
we remember how to laugh, and how, at fifteen,
we ran up the mountain behind home and watched
the eagles soar, feeling their power at the base
of our minds; those birds still move our thoughts
so high we get giddy at the mystery that runs
the world whenever we think of them. At times,
we think about returning home—there is no work
there, and relatives already have trouble making
ends meet, but at least there'd be cousins
to tease. Most of the time, we know such journeys
are impossible, to see us beaten like this would
make our loved ones cry. Here only strangers
see the pain that eats at us like acid eating
into the exposed surfaces on a metal plate,
and these strangers never see us anyway—
only their own visions of what they'll let us be.
It is better to be stared at than known when one has
so little left to give. We look after one another
when we can, and wonder, if the world don't
change soon, how much longer will any of us live.

IT IS IMPORTANT.

On dark nights, when thoughts fly like nightbirds
looking for prey, it is important to remember
to bless with names every creature that comes
to mind, to sing a thankful song and hold
the magic of the whole creation close in the heart,
to watch light dance and know the sacred is alive.
On dark nights, when owls watch, their eyes
gleaming in the black expanse of starless sky,
it is important to gather the medicine bones,
the eagle feathers, the tobacco bundles, the braided
sweetgrass, the cedar, and the sage, and pray
the world will heal and breath feed the plants
that care for the nations keeping the circle whole.
On dark nights, when those who think only of themselves
conjure over stones and sing spells to feed their wills,
it is important to give gifts and to love everything
that shows itself as good. It is time to turn
to the Great Mystery and know the Grandfathers have
mercy on us that we may help the people to survive.
On dark nights, when confusion makes those who envy
hate and curse the winds, face the four directions
and mumble names, it is important to stand
and see that our only work is to give what others
need, that everything that touches us is a holy
gift to teach us we are loved. When sun rises,
and light surrounds life making blessings grow,
it is important to praise its coming, and exhale
letting all we hold inside our lungs travel east
and mix its power with the air; it is important to praise
dawn's power breathing in and know we live in good
relation to all creation and sing what must be sung.

APPROACHING THE MYSTERY

Dark reaches out, whispers from an empty womb.
Moon after moon marks time; the blood tide
washes away the possibility of yet another child.
A woman denies the hunger in her thighs—sings.
A bird's claws pierce her back; wings lift her free
from Earth—she roams farther than any man,
forgets to mourn the passing of her own fertility.
The woman dances in the night; sparks break off stars
and float through space like phosphorus in the tide
until a web of light illuminates the way to go.
The moon calls. The woman dresses all in white,
takes her tools and carves red stone until it grows
into a bowl. She touches Earth, gathers herbs
and bark—leaves an offering. Mist begins to fall,
and plants uncurl and grow. She lights a fire;
bark glows against the curve of stone.
A word is born, and smoke begins to breathe.
The journey begins; the woman prepares her tools and leaves.

HUCKLEBERRY FEAST, WARM SPRINGS NATION, 1979

A bell rings; the welcome song begins.
A chant sung to the rhythm of seven
beaten drums fills the longhouse with music
handed down from times when magic
was taught to people by forces in the wind.
Breath moves beyond speech to pulse
in voice until, through art, it honors nature.
The women enter, berries on their backs
heavy in willow baskets bound around
shoulders with woven burden straps.
These women wear wing dresses and conical hats,
their finest beaded boots and belts in honor
of the entrance of the fruit. They bear this holy
food around the room, their footsteps synchronized
to singers as they pound a patterned beat
as ancient as the sound of blood pumping
through the chambers of the heart and creating
people's first music inside the dark, electric
caverns of their forms. The women circle;
the watching people each swing one hand
as if they ring imaginary bells. A singer
rings the bell again; the women dance
and, with their burdens, turn. The odor
of cedar leaves that keep the fruit contained
rises from basket tops as pungent as the smell
of fresh cut sage. The women turn and lay
their burdens down until each basket rests
upon the mat. Then women as solemn as the moon
greet the waiting people one by one. These women,
in their power, feed the nation what Earth gives.
Chants rise like eagles, and the nation lives.

NIGHT GIVES OLD WOMAN THE WORD

Dark whispers
behind the echo
of the wind. Mind
is trapped by patterns
in the sound.
Night works a spell—
Moon spills her naked light.
Reflected fire illuminates
the ground. The pull
of night words makes Earth-Woman
give off heat. Soil glistens
dampened by her sweat.
Corn seed feels planets turn,
unrolls her root,
prepares to send a shoot
above the dirt. Moon
attracting water in the veins
make corn leaves uncurl
and probe nocturnal air.
The leaves stretch out
to catch the coming dew.
Clan mother, watching,
hears the planets move.
Old, clan mother listens
to the words—all nature
speaks as slowly seasons
turn—marked by the waxing,
waning Moon; messages
become imprinted on old bones.
Earth works in dark
as well as light. Life
moves in constant spiral
through the sky. We plant,
we harvest, and, at last,
we feast. Clan mother listens
and is filled with thanks.
Night murmurs and plants
grow in the fields.
Old Woman hears dark
speak the ancient word.

Dreaming of the Faces That Came To Dance When It Was Cold

AFTER THE INVASION

On dark nights, the women cry together
washing their faces, the backs of their hands
with tears—talking to their grandmother, Moon,
about the way life got confused. Sorrow
comes through tunnels like the wind and wails
inside an empty womb. The need to be cherished,
to be touched by hands that hold sacred objects,
that play the drums and know the holy songs,
rises and moves as certain as the stars.
Women murmur about men who don't sing
when women grind the corn. There are too many
mysteries men learn to ignore; they drink together
and make lewd remarks—defeat makes them forget
to see the magic when women dance, the touch of foot
upon the Earth that mothers them and bears
their bodies across the wide universe of sky.
Men brag how many touch them, who they use,
forget to help women whose love must feed
children that speak of fathers harder to hold
than distant mountains, fathers as inconstant
as the movement of the air. Mothers cook corn
and beans and dream of meat and fish to fill
the storage baskets and the pots. On dark nights,
the women whisper how they love, whisper
how they gave and give until they have no more—
the guilt of being empty breaks their hearts.
They weep for sisters who have learned to hate,
who have gone crazy and learned to hurt
the fragile web that makes the people whole.
Together, women struggle to remember how to live,
nurture one another, and pray that life will fill
their wombs, that men and women will come
to Earth who know that breath is a sacred gift
before the rising sun and love can change
the world as sure as the magic in any steady song.

GATHERING BASKET GRASS

for Mary Nelson

We stood in the muck on the edge
of Shoalwater Bay, the sun making
us sweat as we pulled up the grass
in bunches, triangular stems
popping as they were yanked loose
from the Earth which supports all life.
We bent and stood in rhythmic
motion thinking of our ancestors
plucking the ancestors of this grass
to make baskets, and as we dragged
the heavy bales up the rocks
to the road, we held the image
of the strength of grandmothers carrying
basket materials several miles home;
we held it in our minds. We threw grass
in the car trunk and drove up
the coast to wash off mud and sweat
in the surf before travelling inland.
Now, months have passed since I
sorted and stored these plants.
But every time I open the closet
the smell conjures an image;
I stand with two other Indian women,
my belly full of salmon, and harvest
the fiber used to keep the ancient art alive.

SACRIFICE

The day was scarlet; sun swallowed
the blue expanse; the dark
cavity of the body yawned open
leaving the innards to air; the obsidian
blade cut to the quick though there was
no priest to help; the heart
was dropped in the hands of the gods—
blood spilled on the Earth watering
the ground. At last our sister
gave up her pain; the electricity
quieted and the brain decayed;
the flesh, food to carrion birds,
was picked away. Night came
as hushed as owl's song—no tremors
woke the dead—bone waited
to reveal itself, waited in vain
to be adorned with turquoise
and with shell, to lay steady
in a stone chamber and bless a plaza.
Before the strangers came, she sat
possessed by visions and the intolerable
lightning in the brain that bore all sense
away. Now she continued to make offerings,
blood on thorns that pierced her tongue,
but such things were insubstantial
gifts where so few remembered
the way the spider wove the web
of light together so that magic
was contained in everything. Death
became the offering she hungered
to make; the shame of being human,
of being unable to stop the conquerors
from stealing the ground made it important
to celebrate the miracles of roots and leaves.
When harvest came, she mourned the death

of corn and longed to hurry its rebirth
with her blood: her time came.
She climbed the steps alone and wished
herself away. "Let the people be fed
another year and survive until magic
changes Earth again," she sang
letting stone slit skin. In time
the fear of falling faded; the act
was done, the heart set free.
Her spirit rose and turned toward Earth,
rewound itself in flesh and grew
another name. The corn lay potent
in the seed and was planted—
our sister came to fruit and fed our needs.

THE WOMEN FACULTY AND STAFF RIDE HOME FROM BRITISH COLUMBIA

Driving back through Nooksack County,
trapped in a van full of women
telling stories that are almost true,
gossip laced with metaphors about men
they work with and their wives,
I forget to listen, to care for tales
told out of school about those I barely
know—I let my eyes travel, mind
wander among snowflakes as big
as cats' paws. A dark cloud of starlings
drifts across the road and settles
in a white field. Moving south,
weather changes to rain. Dairy farms
sink into the flood plain, stuck in mud.
Crossing Fish Trap Creek, flooded fields
reflect the sky; gulls fly down to meet
their reflections, walk to the edge of shallow
water, sit in a green field like a flock
of legless paper birds. Women chatter on
facing in; the scenery belongs to me
alone. I watch for names of reservations
where I wish to leave the road—Lummi,
Tulalip, Puyallup, Nisqually—places
I could be just who I am, escape
being one of a different kind. Others
are disappointed to be returning home.
I'm watching names to anyplace
that seems like home pass by.

FURTHER

It is the damp cold that chills the bone.
All around, the leaves of last summer's
raucous miracles of growth decay and feed
the dirt to make next year's growth
possible. Loss is an ephemeral movement,
a mirage awake in the mind; transition
is everywhere and inevitable. The lively
die and change marks out reality. It is
the damp cold that wakes the shiver
in the flesh, makes us come to terms with our
mortality and take the risk
to touch; we know too well the pulse
will cease to beat, the veins become whiskery
webs, paths to nowhere circulating
nothing, and passion can only beam
from the brain an instant against time.
It is the damp chill that teaches
us to celebrate, to build a fire and cry
for ancestors whose loving made us possible,
to cradle children in our arms and pass on
names down a space of time that travels
further than a single human mind can know.

REFLECTIONS ON A VISIT TO THE BURKE MUSEUM, UNIVERSITY OF WASHINGTON, SEATTLE

The things live there, held still in glass cases,
set on pedestals, displayed—the masks,
clothing, boxes, baskets, feast bowls, all
made beautiful so the legends could be told
in ceremonial splendor, so Raven, Killer Whale,
Bear, and Wolf would dance in the circle
of the people to the songs the families possessed.
On those days, masks inlaid with shell of abalone
reflected firelight more subtly than oil
on water makes rainbows in the sun.
Some masks, made to split apart, transformed
characters inside the rhythm of the dance,
a ritual bursting forth that in a moment
altered everything that was. The dancers
dressed in woven aprons and in shawls; cedar
bark ruffs encircled ankles, necks, and wrists
and flapped in wind created by motion contained
inside the vibration of the drums. Song and story
filled the room and beat as steady as the heart
of the people who knew the magic that made
life sacred as it emerged from Changer's mind,
who still perform at feasts how things came to be
and know performance is a gift. Even without the people
to move in them, magic resides in these objects.
The vision of the makers informs the eye.

Around the edges of the room are bones
of long dead creatures who bear exotic names:
Allosaurus, Nannippus, Tylosaurus, Tomistoma-
Machikanese, beasts who roamed before humans were born,
creatures no hunter ever killed. These beings
who have evolved and ceased to have these ancient
forms are mere frames for a past so long dead

we think in awe, in fear, how we could never
fit in such a world. Extinct, they make space
for other bones, for mammoths young enough
to be hunted by ancestors of the makers
of masks and bowls some twelve thousand years
before the carvers held their tools. But bones speak
of death, of things that cannot come to Earth again.
Why should they rest next to the works of men
whose grandsons still explain how we did this
in the old days? The carvers and lovers
of this vision still reside among the people
even though the Europeans who took the land
worked laws to make the old ways die.
Those who made the myth Indians would vanish
as surely as the creatures in the corners
and stairwell of this room, put Native works
of art together with these long gone bones—
the vision of the makers informs the eye.

MEDICINE BEARER

The Medicine Bearer comes like a red
apparition; he knows the plants and the time
of the moon for gathering magic rooted
to a murmuring Earth that makes it possible
to be. He bruises branches with his teeth
and tells by taste what young shoots
and roots will make the proper tea
to heal a heavy heart. He gathers things
to himself which sparkle and whisper
in the wind of another's breath. Even
in the dark, light glints and his presence
is revealed by power lumbering bearlike
over ground. At noon, he arrives and tells
the one who cried four days the words
to say when preparing to make medicine
to help the people needing to grow strong.
Love shapes the lessons he teaches
as he dances on this spinning planet,
his footsoles keeping rhythm to a pulse
beating steady like the song of a great drum.

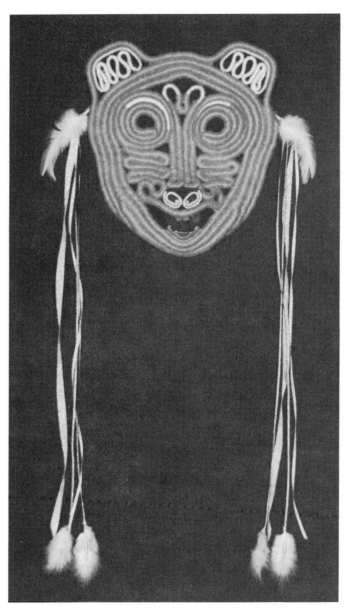

Medicine Bearer

AN ONONDAGA SITS IN INTERNATIONAL
CHILDREN'S PARK, SEATTLE

February
    Back home it snows, every branch
    is heavy with ice; trees pop,
    drop limbs, strew them across the ground.
    Sap won't run for another month,
    and sweetness seems like it may never rise
    in the maple; last year's syrup
    is almost gone. People hold one another
    between blankets and dream
    sun will grow near enough to make them
    warm. They trust touch and time
    will make things well; they stoke the stove.

    In Seattle, no further south, I sit
    in a park where bushes blossom—
    purple flowers explode on bare branches,
    a contrast as startling as silk
    against steel. On the next bench,
    a Navaho from Arizona and a Chinese
    born in Hong Kong share a bottle.
    We sit, huddled in our coats,
    watch sparrows glide through fog,
    land on branches making petals
    vibrate with the promise of Spring.

April

At home, at last, the snow melts;
only gullies, the shadowy spaces
under trees hold spongy patches
turned grey long ago. Relatives
write even the nights are warmer.
The sweet sap has ceased to flow;
everyone gave thanks in the longhouse
and sang the old songs around the drum
marking the change of seasons. The pulse
grows quicker and grandmothers
brew sassafras tea to thin the blood.

Here, the purple flowers have faded,
and new leaves unfold. Cherry trees
bloom and the smell travels on the breeze
haunting sense. Today, grey for the first
time in a week, the park is empty;
no old friends come to talk; no children
slide or climb on the smiling bronze dragon.
Today, in the midst of a Spring
that has been blooming for three months,
I remember to marvel how far I've come
by following the path of my elder brother, Sun.

NOT SENSE

The tongue shapes and molds sound. Speech
becomes sensation in the mouth vibrating
on the palate and the teeth—touch
done with more than fingertips transmutes
itself to rhythm in the ear. Words outleap
meaning and turn into a way to move.
We speak the names that objects will become.
Voice wakes the light, and we begin to see
the shadows leaves can make against the wood.
We say Earth spins, and suddenly the clouds
move like ghosts of old ones bringing rain
that loves the growing things upon the ground.
I listen to your breath against my skin
and wait for you to name the way you feel,
to tell me where you've been and where you go,
to find the shape of things we share and have
to give. I lean and whisper words to let you see
the beauty that I watch when I'm with you.
My tongue slips nimbly past my teeth
and finds lips ready to caress
the line of small round scars that mark
your cheek. Nothing mars the surface
of your skin; what is is graceful and words
could never see it any other way. I watch with senses
more perceptive than my eyes, and let you touch me
more than once or twice. Your voice says little;
sound echoes in my senses like the wind.
You fill the dark passages of form with murmurs
that inhabit me until I learn it's sound not sense
that fills the world, that keeps me warm.

TO JOSEPH, WHO IS NEVER GONE:

Though you've been dead for more than a decade,
I still feel your touch as certain as the touch
of wind breathing in the ends of my hair. I turn
and mourn, caught in a sorrow as useless
as a broken bucket, a vessel that leaks
and can no longer bear up under the strain.
I can remember how you sang and painted my hair part
red when you took me, a virgin, and I bled,
the first woman you ever loved for the first time.
You made me full, and after you went to sleep,
I drew the ridge of your face with my fingertip
and memorized the shadows eyelashes made
on your cheeks. When I close my eyes, you come to me
stumbling from memories so old that dust
hangs in the sunlight of my dreams. I no longer
have any need to whisper your name; old ghosts
call to me, and I awake caught in an ecstasy
as ephemeral as the veins of leaves that rot
away over an interminable winter. Tears could
never wash away my grief; it grew into the very bones
that bear my love. An insatiable hunger sits
in my flesh; I can never taste the salt
of your lips. Like a salmon, I swim hard against
the current, but no one will ever fertilize
my eggs—the stream is silted up, and new life
suffocates. Sometimes, I face into the wind and pray
the world will change. I give away everything I have
and long to be empty, to erase our history,
to forget holding you, your skull cracked,
bone moving where it should have been solid
in my hand. Nothing ever makes it possible
to wish you away. Your dying bound me
to you in a world where what was can never age.

THE INEVITABLE

for my sister

At night, sleep takes me across fields
flying through dreams as vivid
as flowers exploding in slow motion.
Red petals float away like blood
dissolving in a river, and light
shivers and is gone. The moon
rises pregnant with grief—rises
mourning too many stillborn beings
poisoned by chemicals suffocating
the surface of Earth. Suffocating,
Earth turns and slowly finds the light.
Vision shimmers; the eye opens.
In the morning, the sad bird comes
calling—its low moan telling
about death waking from a dream
to kill another relative—death
dragging days through empty space
to teach me of a loss I don't want to suffer—
but it's coming anyway.

SINGING OUT THE GHOSTS

Singing out the ghosts, I unlearn weeping,
forget to dream about dead relatives
sharing a dark dance at the bottom
of the sea. I learn to listen as the birds
split light with their sound.
The owls let go, forget to dream my name.
I hold my breath in my hands—the pulse
of air swells and recedes like waves spreading
life on the shore. Singing out the ghosts,
I give up thoughts of my mother's corpse
changing color, growing nails and hair,
bleeding rot into the sweet groaning ground.
Bones become pure, allow me to be; I let
the living touch me and wash me with their tears.

FALLING, GLORIA LOOKS UP

for G.M.Y.

Decay sets in before death as nerve cells
rot away; sensation becomes a stranger—
Limbs prickle as though the thistle bloomed
inside the skin; the skin itself is numb;
touch reveals little about the texture of the world.
Walking becomes difficult; legs stumble,
feel unattached; she cannot find her feet
unless she looks; she steps across the floor
as though wading through mud and becomes
exhausted; she collapses in a chair knowing
there is no way to look normal standing up.
The body is betrayed; time is measured
by loss—she becomes sensitive to sad events;
today she dropped her fork three times
and wept at the sight of food in her lap—
her whole body shivered like poplar leaves;
tears shimmered on her face and ran
down her chin dropping on her breasts,
a strange salt rain. She comes to think
of change as a flower rotting in a vase
with no one to throw it out. Only tenderness,
a visit from grown children who hold her, the touch
of her husband in bed distract her enough
so she can remember why she is still alive.

Conversation becomes an exercise in memory;
"Remember when I could still walk the beach,
the time we found the agate with the dark red
lines that put bars around the sun when I held it
to your eye. Remember when I rode the grey mare
with the face like a sheep and we saw the hawk
dive, his soft body a blur suddenly caught on wings,
feathers arching against the blue. Remember . . ."

Her children learn to cherish her past
as surely as their futures. Alone they cry
that nothing lasts—life seems as tenuous
as snowflakes melting in the hand, elaborate
patterns breaking down before the eye. Gloria
tells them of a hundred yesterdays that time
has swept away. Alone she struggles to cope
with losing simple skills. The day she can no longer
button her blouse, she cries, resolve melting;
she feels herself slipping away, no frame
of bone strong enough to keep her from falling
to the floor. She lay and looked at the ceiling
seeing the shadows of leaves in the light
from the window as delicate brush paintings
transformed to moving pictures in the wind, the present
moment contained in images as startling as the pain.

EDGES

In dreams, I dance all night
around the drum; I pray
on mountaintops at rising sun;
hummingbirds resist the mountain
wind, touch flower throats with narrow
sticky tongues. The planet whirls
and raptors soar and dive;
creation wakes the wit; I am alive.

I wake and plot to turn myself
in bed. I grasp behind my knee
and move my leg. My body slowly
works its way around. Outside,
the moon moves through the starry
sky. I lay between the sheets,
contain the sound; my heart beats
steady, knows the ground is flying
faster than feet can find a way
to go now that nerve cells no longer
recognize the will to climb to high
ground and touch the edges of the sky.

HÉN; IÁH; TÓKA' NÓN:WA.

Death comes drenching me to the bone,
a drop at a time like rain falling
slow and steady; cells swell
and burst; nerves alter, and scars
block pathways to old possibilities
as surely as dams keep fish
from going upstream to spawn.
Some days, *kahséhtha' akweriàkon;*
kón:nis invisible that change in sense
that marks the passing of dreams
that can never come to be. I refuse
to cry and think it best to act
on the instant, to give each moment
its special weight, notice the way
light shifts defining the movement
of minutes that bury what could move
in me. I give up the desire to dance
one more season around the drum;
I grow content to feel its rhythm
move my pulse one beat, then another,
while others slap footsoles on the path
I used to keep. You ask me, honestly,
can I face years of this continual loss?
   Hén. Iáh. Tóka' nón:wa.

Hén; iáh; tóka' nón:wa: Yes; no; maybe
kahséhtha' akweriàkon: I hide something in my heart
kón:nis: I make

LIGHT SHAKES

Light shakes among waves, reflects
off facets cut in fluid by the wind.
The surface rocks and fish leap
and dive into a weedy world
that breathes through gills
as startling as the plumes
of egrets grown inside chambers
of flesh covered with scales. Dark
among rocks, sand dollars bristle
and know light lines as delicate
as threads wound and bound in lace,
light sinking from the surface
of the Sound to create elaborate
patterns on the sand. This world
spins between continents careening
through the stars, a chariot to rock
us in our dreams and teach us
how to bear the pain of being
only human in bodies so momentary
that our bones grow naked before all
our love is spent and gone away.

DAWN DOWN EAST

Day breaks against the shore, washes away
darkness that hides patterns in the sand;
sun rises glittering through the spray;
light outlines the creatures of the land.
The circle of creation turns around; life
is supported by everything that is; thanks
fills those minds that hold vision ripe
as Earth mothering plants which root on flanks
of hills as rich as flesh damp with sweat
shining slippery under simple beads of dew.
The song of praise awakes, expands the quiet
rhythm of the pulse; the heart beats new
tunes inside the flesh, the heat of waking
with the continent a sacred undertaking.

MOVING THROUGH DARK

Moving through dark and light, the planet turns;
the universe continues to expand—
The sun careens through heavens, and it burns.

Fire overcomes inertia, and it earns
the strength to define direction in the land:
moving through dark and light, the planet turns.

Change is inevitable, the person learns
motion is constant in ways no creature planned.
The sun careens through heavens, and it burns,

creates a spiral path the Earth discerns.
We whirl through space and try to understand
why moving through dark and light, the planet turns.

We move about caught in our concerns;
forget the stage we move upon is grand.
The sun careens through heavens, and it burns.

Time travels on, the person just sojourns;
we hardly sense the motion as we stand
moving through dark and light. The planet turns.
The sun careens through heavens, and it burns.

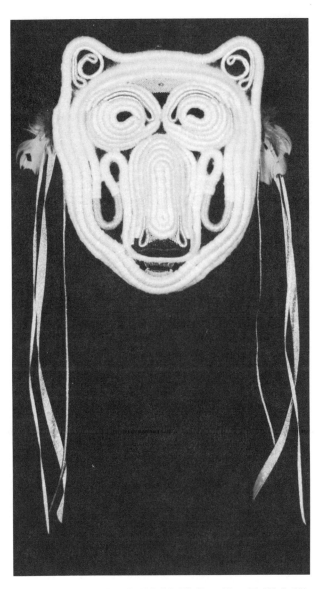

KO-KO-KO-IO-TI Goes East To Visit His
Younger Brother Eirhar

CREATION IS THE SONG

Light filters through branches and leaves,
reflects off particles of dust,
makes air visible; the breeze
floats specks too small to sense with touch.

Earth motion stirs the rhythm of the wind;
music dances—breath against the skin.
Sound rattles tiny bones inside the ear;
sensation wakes the nerves; we learn to care.

Moment moves toward revelation like a pond
reflecting clouds around the waxing moon
while depths remain the dark and glistening home
for fish and ferment rocking on the ground.

The circle of creation knows our name;
we watch its magic rule despite the harm
that men forgetting sacred patterns bring
to Earth steering paths around the stars.

Miracles rise as simple as the stones
which murmur hidden secrets to the sun;
we rise and grow in what we know:
creation is the song which haunts our tongues.

TSOOYES BEACH, MAKAH NATION, 1981

At land's edge one feels the planet whirl—
water, pulled as moon circles Earth,
whips itself into a froth and rolls
against the shore. Wind spits; salt spices air
which moves, rises, buoys up birds
who glide, see food sparkle in the tide
and dive. Near the horizon, the sun grows
enormous and slips from view as the continent
turns toward the dark, infinite universe
of stars. Moon comes pregnant into view; round
as the sun, she sails across the sky, her face,
shadows cast by craters on her crust,
that stone mirror of the orb whose fire makes
possible our lives. And I, standing on sand
washed by an ocean moving with the spheres,
share this miracle with a seal floating
between waves. We watch one another drift
through space moving faster than sensation
ever tells, the reflection of the way we spin
as palpable as electricity humming in our living cells.

THE RETURNING

It is these long journeys to the heart
of the continent, moving too fast
thirty thousand feet above the planet
that leave me longing to whisper
to medicine roots that send shoots
as fine as hair for miles to anchor
themselves to ground. The body feels
strangely out of context. I desire
to see agates sparkle among cirrus clouds
stretched out like endless waves
washing no shore. I grow lonely
for the dirt, lonely for the horizon
that marks time in relation to sun
and stars as it spins across the sky.
Up here, there are momentary miracles:
outside Denver, a lake turns golden
as it mirrors sun; clouds and mountains
move together creating atmosphere
for one another as Earth arcs through space.
But this journey is a pause in normal
breathing; a movement through thin air
kept away by delicate walls and will,
this distant place is not meant to sustain
the flesh. Even birds fly miles
below, knowing the plants creating
air can only send their life-giving
gift so far. It is the returning to Earth
that lets the skin contain the pulse,
the returning to Earth that feeds the muscle
of the heart and makes love possible.

BUS RIDE, OMAHA, NOVEMBER, 1977

for my father

Rising and diving into the flock
of scattering starlings,
the hawk wheels, wind pressing
on wings, buoying him up—
starlings regroup, veer left
as the high hawk, a mere dot
in the prairie sky, swoops again
toward the intense knot
of small dark birds darting
in controlled terror,
an attempt to escape
the death of one of their number.
And I, riding a bus
through this green city,
almost stand to announce
the miracle outside the moving window,
but see fellow travellers
caught in the landscape of thought
and don't interrupt, spare them
the witness of nature
in its raw agility—
the dull thud of death snatching
a small body in mid-air.
I settle in my seat,
living a tenuous life
that quickens the pulse,
my bird breath measuring out
this momentary leap toward infinity.

TO TEACH THE WIT

It is the sense of constant motion
that is most amazing when one sits
silent watching light vibrate,
Earth move in relation to the sun
spinning through space, the web
of the spider becoming bright beads
of dew for moments before the shadows
cast by the turning planets eclipse the vision.
The need to need at all is lost
in a thicket as time ceases to tick,
flows like water carving the sides
of mountains, shaping change
on a schedule no human designs.
Irony reveals the joke caught
in the flesh, blind to the breath
of thunder-beings whipping up storms
with their fiery tongues. We move
in the dark for half our lives,
forget to use our second sense
to watch the miracles unfold;
murmuring generations enrich the dust
with their deaths to make birth possible.
In such a context, care is attention
to details simple enough to teach
the wit to love the momentary pulse.

FALL

The sun rides high travelling farther
from this northern place each day.
The Earth grows cooler like a stone
taken from near the fire. I go to bed
full of hope I won't wake to shrivelled
leaves, that the squash will grow bigger
and their yellow flowers will bear pollen-
covered bees for one more changing
of the moon. The days grow shorter,
and the inevitable end glides in
with the shift of planets wheeling
according to some magic that makes
things thaw and grow in Argentina
as all goes dormant here, so Earth
is fed, made fertile, by the rot
of frost-killed plants. Life is made
possible by death and the movement
of stars through a universe we barely
comprehend. Soon the work of storing
food for winter will be—in an instant—
over, and winter will be here to test
our skill to survive another year, until,
at last, our season to be turned under comes,
and we feed Earth, who supports all life,
with our flesh fed by vegetable flesh.

AND WAKE

Incandescent fire evaporates substance;
the cloud billows, spews dust and ash.
Dark swallows dark; the strange unknown
absorbs the center; a cavern too vast
to contain the sense of loss reveals
its mouth. Endless space rocks sand
and stone. Soon, there is no one to know.
But madness such as this need never be;
we need not build bombs and still
the breath; love creates new bones clothed
in tender flesh, and we can share
the gifts of Earth and touch. Those people
who have forgot, need to turn in an embrace
and hold small children until they know
death comes in its own good time without
their meddling. They must let go of power
until they unlearn terror and the desire
to control another's destiny. Torture cannot
teach generosity; the dawn must, by coming,
reveal that it is day and shadows dance
because light travels making magic
that circles with the planet 'round the sun.
It is unwise to hoard the bombs and guns;
let people plant the fields and feed the hunger
in the gut; choose those who give the most
as leaders and disarm the violent instruments
that haunt the dreams until lovers lose
their wits and think that love has grown
impossible. Let plants transmute the light
that we may digest wisdom in the seed and wake
the rhythm of creation that beats in us.

Medicine Bear

Gail Tremblay is of Onondaga/Mic Mac and French Canadian ancestry. She is a poet, an artist, and a member of the faculty at The Evergreen State College (Olympia, WA). She works hard, loves her work and her students, and is never bored.

The text of this book was typeset in Palatino by the
Corvallis Typesetting Company, Corvallis, Oregon.
The book was printed at
McNaughton & Gunn, Ann Arbor, Michigan.